Memory Tree

Memory Tree
Gareth Culshaw

HENDON PRESS

Published 2022 by
Hendon Press
21 Wykeham Road,
Hendon,
London
NW4 2TB

ISBN 978-1-7397785-0-7

Gareth Culshaw hereby asserts his moral right to be identified as the author of this book.

British Library Cataloguing-in-Publication Data.
A catalogue record for this book is available from the
British Library.

Designed & Typeset by Utter
Printed and bound by Imprint Digital
Cover image: 'A Man Walking to Work, Treharris, South Wales 1977'
© Robin Weaver

Acknowledgements
I am grateful to the editors of the publications some of these first appeared in: *Wellington Street Review*, *The Poeming Pigeon*, *Arachne Press Winter Solstice Anthology*, *Sunday Tribune*, *Milk & Beans*, *Abridged*, *Stand*, *Salamander*, *Smoke*, *Dear Reader*, *Slush Anthologies – Friendship & Childhood*, *Nine Pens Hair Anthology*, and *Unpublishable*.

Special mention to Lydia Allison who curated April's showcase with the Poetry Business, and for publishing my poem 'The Old Lad By Us'.

Special thanks to Carol Ann Duffy & Manchester Met for accepting poems towards the Write Where We Are Now Project during Covid Lockdown.

Contents

To my grandparents Hetty, Elsie, Joe & Tom

Sometimes I Get Up Early to Find the Light

I walk under the arch entering the moon.
Stars become gorse flowers with each footstep.
In the growing light a horse gives me a single
wellie look. Molehills, inside-out potholes,
and a tree stands as a rusty nail. I feel the weight
of last night seep through my mouth as a breeze
gives nerves to a holly.

Somewhere in my head an owl lingers, draws
the cupboard dark to an end. Sheep whip-cream
themselves out of the ground. An eyebrow
of sunlight breaks clear of the dreams I left
behind in bed. A woodpecker taps down
the tacks on winter's lid. Whaleback hills
rise out of the wood's canopy.

Someone brings the sky back to earth
as a dog's bark becomes a flapping tin sheet.
Two tractors unzip the road. A jogger
knocks a human out of my eyes. I scratch a piece
of toast off my head, spread breakfast yolk
across the horizon. Soon my face will appear
for the birds to alarm call as I enter their beaks.

A Neighbour from Across the Field

His age pushes against the skin as tree roots
under tarmac. There's a breeze lost in his hair
as he mallets another year into the ground.
The pigs he owned are now packaged on shelves
he walks past in the local Aldi. He reshapes a field
his father grew in a 1960's beard. The same father
who showed him light in a water butt is only
there because of the sun, and to start a bonfire you
have to find the fire. The thumping sound carries across
his shoulder girdle as electricity between pylons.
You hear the tractor burp in cereal mornings as it drags
across his pothole breath. He spits quick like a spark
of sparrowhawk, eats sandwiches before they go out
of date, drinks milk with a coo-shaped mouth.

The chainsaw he's tied to silence disturbs pheasants
who hide inside their feathers, turns a jackdaw
into a flock, closes my window as I read. Sometimes
I pass him on the road as he drives himself to the end,
our eyes binocular what we know of each other.
His mouth, wordless, until the pigs return in spring.
And a charm of goldfinch detach from his frown,
buckle his stare.

The Dog Walker That Keeps Our Village Alive

They both move along the path as car headlights on a dark road.
Her face looks like the first sun on seeing its light
reflect off a tree. Her eyebrows paint horizons.

The dog walks alongside, wags a tail found in a hedgerow.
She whistles bird song and tuts at the litter that brings colours
to dilute the country path. They're both retired now, using

their living hours to unsettle clouds, or croak puddle ice
that comes in winter. Sometimes the dog will chase a rabbit,
catch a squirrel in its eyelids, bring autumn leaves to her feet.

She giggles at joggers who use the same distance, but ignore
the gap between land and sky. I watched her zip a coat
and a crow flew out of her. Her hair is a nursery rhyme,

and she combs it with slate-smooth fingers on the doorstep.
The postman ignores her house though puts her post in the letterbox.
She has been alone for seventeen years, hiding within her glance.

Some say her eyes can make the moon blink. I bumped into her
once on a spring morning, and something fell from her features,
made me drink two cups of tea.

Waiting at the Bus Stop with a Girl I Had Never Seen

Her ears twitched as radars searching for alien sounds.
I saw makeup smudged over her Vimto-swigging lips.
She wore yesterday, spoke into a phone with a muted tongue.
The bus was late. Two dogs sniffed the air through a gate.
Swifts busied themselves with chicane moves below clouds.
I had my hands in pockets like a golfer waiting his turn to putt.
She finished the call, put her phone back in her mouth.
Her eyes a mole's when digging through soil. I was going
to ask her if everything was fine, but her stilettos made me
weary. Perfume coughed from her chest. Mascara kept
the sunlight out of her eyes. The bus was late. Cars filled
petal silence with brake sounds and arguing rubber.

I looked down the road for the bus; nothing came by except
a pick-up truck full of fence panels. The driver's beard
made from the death of someone he loved. She got up,
walked away from the stop with ballerina calves,
tennis player thighs, and left me to watch the swifts.
I never saw her again, that's if you ignore the day,
I watched a blackbird through my binoculars.

The Old Lad by Us

He whistles with a walking stick these days, grabs a tan off
the digesting sun. Rolls up a newspaper for a square pocket.
Catches butterflies with his eyelashes. Shaves his soles along
a road built for tractors. Spits into potholes through a badger-dug
mouth. Gone are the days of Larsen traps, pheasant food,
and bullets for sparrowhawks. A scratch of stubble grinds
out of a jaw too big for a face. Nostril hair dangles
as spider legs on a brick. Triangular sun rays fill
his bald patch with a light he only sees in his moonlit yard.
A limp falls out of him every six steps. The sandy brown coat
fits over a shoulder girdle with a grip he shows to rabbit fur.
His wife is alive though keeps her voice for the AGA.
They have a Land Rover and three grandchildren. Feed all
with frowns and stutter. A laburnum grows at the end of his garden,
masts a summer he forgets when picking tomatoes.
Winter hides in his left eye, flickers in a sty that lingers still.
Every morning he puts down this road with a biscuit-dunked tongue.
If I see him dog walking, I feel a coldness that makes me check
my fly is up. He swallows you whole if you haven't had breakfast.
When he's gone, I look back, watch him bend a corner.
Hear the silence in the living.

The Builder

He keeps cutting away at the mound of sand, scoops
a plate of cement, and throws in tap water. His teeth grind
with each load, bring veins to his forehead, show clots
of winter he scrolls in fag paper. His father's face glances
off his chin, rolls down his sleeve as he turns another shovel.
Clouds pilfer sunlight above a hairline he last saw
in the bathroom mirror of his mother's house. Rain pickles
itself on tarmac, bricks lie in the shoebox of themselves.
A spirit level shows him the earth is not the balance of life
he got told in Sunday School. A cross hangs from his neck,
dangles bird flight, that a buzzard watches in the sky.
The weary drum shakes a breeze that flickers oak leaves.
A KitKat wrapper falls from his pocket, twitches in a puddle.
He gives a sigh, winks an eye to shake off the site's iron.
Rain itches away ginger sunlight, trips up a church clock's bong.
He fills another wheelbarrow, pushes it with tight hips,
bundles himself over the potholes and cambers he brought
from home. Rests it down with pallbearer hands.
Rolls another skin of lung, whittles it away in his father's mouth.

I Was Half His Size

Those days in the cemetery walking along the paths
that were being forced up by the roots of trees.

Marble gravestones inched their way to the floor,
became drawbridges for sunlight.

The tap that dripped when tight, gushed when open.
Pots of flowers filled, then brought back to her date.

I was half the height of you back then. Wondered what
the other half would bring. There was silence and a vast

sky above. Her chiselled name stung the marble. I never
trod on her lawn thinking maybe one day she would

come back. But all the time you stood there knowing
that the other half of my growth was the slowest lived.

And felt the same day, after day, after day.

I Climbed a Tree with a Kitkat in Hand

When I was a boy I climbed trees, broke a KitKat on the tallest
branches. My fingers grabbed twiglets, scaled the ribs of my youth.
The higher I went the smaller my parents became.
They looked like ants when they shouted at me to come back down.
I wanted to see if the clouds were alive instead of floating
foam in the Sunday night bath. My legs aped themselves
until a tiptop landed in my pocket from a friend down below.
I sucked the winter out of it, then carried on until rooftops became
driveways for birds. The moon, a digestive biscuit on a table.
The tree drilled into the ground as I reached for its canopy.
My hands gripped the bark, and I felt like the cat that climbs
the neighbour's Christmas tree. People watched, shouted words
muffling my ears until they popped out in farts. A summer sky
seemed touchable. I pawed the open air, and heard the snap of a twig.
Bent the spine of my childhood, waited for an adult one to grow.
The top, as thick as a dwarf conifer. I glanced up, heard
a whistle in my armpit. I started to take myself back down
with the speed of a pylon painter. The ground filled my pocket,
and the weight of my parents' tongues coaxed me to the end,
until I felt the grip of a hand on my earlobe.

Ink for Blood

Some nights we sat like chicks in a nest.
TV fed us light and a dictionary of words I could not hear.
Mother was in her caravan years as he nudged himself
to allotment age. I only saw their faces when the curtains
broke free of darkness. We stayed here each night.
Hours later, morning happened. A butter-silk sun smoothed
the living room walls, hid shadows that lived behind
embossed wallpaper. Mother sat again, but this time,
the remote control lay as a dead soldier in a field.
His radio cavitied the kitchen, as we both looked through
the living room window, watched heads bob along the top
of the hedgerow. Turtle-eyed, Mother checked the clock,
waited to tilt her head back for white submarines
the doctor subscribed her each month. Even now,
I'm not sure if I was meant to be there. Similar to snowfall
in a desert. The radio turned off and a newspaper
sneaked in noise. He opened up the living room
like a lumberjack splitting a log. Mother moved her
ladybird-shaped feet. Coats zipped up to biscuit tin
the warmth of the house. They walked with bear-like steps,
locked the front door in case I felt like going out.
A quarter of a century I lived within their mouths, heard
voices canal barge into my ear. Waited for something
to hold onto. A daffodil that grew through the tarmac
with ink for blood.

Sunlight

The first time I saw the sunlight was peeling
an orange in the kitchen.

Though a shade soon appeared as he turned the page
of his Daily Mirror.

I looked out into the garden, saw a concrete floor suffocate
childhood memories of playing ball with Mother.

He whistled in my ear, buttered a bread crust on a table
that balanced on his lap.

Mother sat in the dying room. Watched television through
the gap of his lips.

A radio trickled words, filled a cup of tea, before his left
hand stirred away another day.

As I moved, my feet palmed my body across a floor
now lost beneath a carpet.

I left this room to his walnut tut, entering Mother's eyeline,
before throwing peeled sunlight into the bin.

The Fireplace

I will never forget that time
when the wind fell down
the chimney. The sky
had caved in someplace,
and its contents fell into our
home. The winter's ash
leapt for cover and the noise
carried on into the hallway.
The wind itself hit our shins
and shivered our skin
like a breeze over the sea.
We should have known
there and then that the fireplace
was an usher.

Roscoe

He had hobnailed boots under his pillow,
took the clouds with him every day.
His eyes sat back in his skull as if life
had stunned him. He walked between
his home and garage with a tight lip,
'F' word cocked, body shadowless
in summer. We goaded him when he
came round, his legs too thin to move
quicker than walking. He had his past
in his pocket and scrunched it up
with his hands. You would hear him
swearing in his living room
when we walked past bouncing
a football. The labour he had done
filled his bones, tore his sinews,
and diluted his skin. The pain
he suffered came out of his mouth
like blood from a fresh wound.

The Bricklayer Who Laid Books

I knew a bloke who was a bricklayer,
but rumour has it he was also a librarian.
When he built a wall, he stood the bricks
on edge. Put bookmarks between joints
and he gave words to the brick's spines.
He once built a house on top of a hill.
When the wind came the house fell
back as the bricks were laid upright.
The owners propped it back up with books
left behind by the bricklayer. He lost
his trade when the library asked for a wall
to be built between two rooms.
When he finished, they checked his work,
and found he had stacked books
from floor to ceiling. He said he ran out
of bricks so used them instead.
He retired early, ran a bookshop in the local
market. Stall holders would see him
with his spirit level during the day levelling
out his stock. Sometimes he was seen mixing
mortar behind his till, slapping it between
books he wanted to sell two-for-one.

Upside Down, Inside Out

He wore a hat on each foot.
Put socks on his hands.
When the neighbours saw him
he said he got dressed with his
eyes closed.

Some said when his wife died
he found out who he wasn't.
The pool cue he carried between pubs
stayed in the hallway, leaned against
the wall like an umbrella.

He still washed her clothes
and hung them out on the line.
If the postman knocked he answered
him through the bay window.
Took his post via his mouth.

If it rained he swapped his hat
and socks. If the sun came out he
swapped them back. But if frost
came he didn't know what to do,
so left them at home on the sofa.

The Miner and His Wife

There was a time when he cut his hedge with his wife's hands.
Her tongue combed clouds that painted the matted hair
on his head. He filled bin bags with snipped summer months,
brushed away children's feet as they played on the road.
He never smoked unless his wife passed him one through
the two conifers that hung a shade over their bay window.
He'd worked as a coal miner for fifty-four years. Bringing
underground dust up the road every evening after work.
We watched him walk home as beans on toast filled our youth.
His feet tick-tocked, and almond eyes he'd grown after school
clung to the edge of his skull, ready to fall off into the abyss.
They lived in number three all their life. Cut a squared lawn
on the first day of each month. Cleaned windows with newspapers,
hoovered up letters from a postman, raked away autumn leaves
that ached to be back on the twig of things. His wife bore
two cats, fed them with a teaspoon on a red-coloured doorstep.
Pigeons sat on gutters he bought from TEXAS Homestore.
They cooed until dark, raising the sun from inside their throats.
He shot them with a pellet gun as he enjoyed the darkness,
knowing he won't see his wife until hometime.

She Mops Away the Grime of Her Life

Her mop angles the body she found in the shadow
of her mother. Red floor tiles gleam as she smudges
away footsteps of school children.
A ceiling fan whirls words she has in her chewing gum.
A fly taps the window pane, shows the boundaries
of her life. She pushes through grime, cleans coffee
stains off her teeth. The grey hair she started
to grow after her third child climbs to her shoulder.
She opens the corridor door, sighs like a deflating football.
The bags under her eyes hold late hours sat
in front of a muted TV. A teacher walks by, leaves
his Lynx deodorant breath in her hair. He mocks
the tiles with his tippy-tappy shoes. She glances back
at his trouser belt, sees the coastline of a peninsula
she was born on. The bucket holds fluorescent light,
bobs as she pushes it with her foot. Two children
giggle as they run by after doing extra homework.
She hears them lost in her earwax as she swipes
away another hour of work. She dunks into the mop,
pulls it back out like a digestive biscuit. Her mobile
pings, shines a text off her eldest, a ring-binder tut
escapes her mouth.

The Old Lady That Whispers Her Life to Her Cat

She opens her biscuit tin with a hand made in a sewing factory.
Yesterday's breeze cues through the open window, flickers
a corner of last week's newspaper. A kitchen light holds colours
bought at TK Maxx. Steam escapes her mug of tea, climbs
to an Artex ceiling. Custard creams are bricks in a fallen wall
as she picks one up to dunk.
Her cat sits within fur found along a streetlight road.
They purr to each other with hoover vibrations. Catch sun rays
between their eyes when the Old Lady butters Jacobs Crackers.
A neighbour pops round three times a week, brings soup
and unsliced bread. They share cups of tea with dancefloor hands,
bite a biscuit crumb found on their cardigan sleeves.
Swap words found in the local newspaper's wordsearch.
He leaves if his wife sees him through her own double-glazed eyes.
Hears her tut in the back of a Lozenge throat. Unfolding a war-dieted
body he grabs an Asda-bought curtain to pull himself back to height.
The Old Lady turns on the kettle, lets it boil twice before pouring
away another afternoon. Her cat sits on a pile of magazines,
allows his shape to bring curves to the four walls.
She watches a crow, but off he has to go, like her youth, gone.

Simon

As he walked, his fringe moved as a For Sale sign in the wind.
He bought his feet off another kid back in school twenty years ago.
Now he limps his way around shopping centres of the local town.
On his shoulder hangs a leather bag that keeps daily medication
safe from the rain and eyes of locals.
He never knew who he wanted to be in life but thought a banker
would go well considering his soap-soft hands. Pencilled lips
photo frame his words, hold snail damp after a morning whiskey.
Their colour continues on from the beetroot he ate with his salad
last night. Sometimes he whistles a tune his gran played
on the record player during her husband's Bible reading.
His wife is his husband and they live in a fridge shaped house.
The neighbour's ask "why play tennis on the lawn
when the measurements indicate a squash court".
He grows flowers in the house guttering to give birds something
to eat during winter. After tea, him and his husband talk
to each other through open bedroom windows, vape their words
until a cloud hovers over the roof. Then they close for the owls
hoot to spin the garden to darkness under a sky.

I Deliver Newspapers to a Man of Medals

I cut the cheese with an arm that knows the throat.
My thatch of hair holds frost as spiderwebs in a shed.
The newspaper boy never knocks, only pushes the papers
in with a librarian touch. The sound of paper falling
is like a body felled by a burst of bullets.
I mutter as a horse in the rain as I leave the cheese.
My form breaks up the darkness of the coat-hanger hallway.

Opening the door, the boy sees the scars on my cheeks
as I flick off the moonlight. I unfold a five-pound note
and my hands shake out youth lost in the deserts of Iraq.
I look into his eyes, find a bullet swirling as a fly
in a flushed toilet. He holds the bag's weight with a gallant
smile and uncombed fringe. The fresh look he wears shows
the life I could've lived. I read the headlines, spit a shell-
shocked face, hear the kettle click in the kitchen.

My frown closes his eyelids. I nod at the change in his hand.
He turns away, and I slip into a shadow, wait with the cheese
knife. Hear him snip the latch leaving me to the moon.

We Played with Beer Cans

I played footie on Howard's Field for the last time
as a twenty-two-year-old. Beer kept the sun off our backs
and made the ball lighter on the head. With each kick
a new muscle felt old. Gone were the days of watching
time or rubbing away smudge marks off our joggies.
The trainers could be replaced next payday. Half-time
was longer as we sat with flexed elbows to prop us up.
Texts pinged during the game like disturbed birds in hedging.
Cans, crushed by a foot, after being emptied of their weight.
Burps rumbled out of us. For a moment we polluted the air.
We never kept score or who was winning, but fed ourselves
with sunlight, gossip, and laughter. Forearms became slabs
of salmon on a market stall. Our noses flaked like the memories
I had of this place. The field, smaller now: the bottom could
be explored without going down. The divots we made, scrapes
in the grass, all grown back to level off with the sky.

He was Never a Gardener

When I saw you raking the soil
with the long wooden handle
and rounded back, saw sweat
from every push and drag.

I knew you were not a gardener.

You hated the mower and pushed
it in such a way I thought you
were imagining it going over a cliff.
The spade stood formal against
the house. The hard edge threatened
to cut the world in half when you
put your foot on it.

I knew you were never a gardener.

Hedge clippers snipped away
the summer days leaving lost time
all over the floor. I had to help
brush up the unwanted.

You held the black bin bag
while I scooped up the trimmings.
We were at our closest then, filling
up what we knew we didn't need.

But I knew you were never a gardener.

A Saturday Afternoon Before Adulthood

The sky pasted itself over the pitch.
People stood up, ate pies, hotdogs,
torched the natter with fag ends.
Footballers ran up and down,
stretched sleep out of legs, rotated
arms to windmill their energy.

Someone kicked a football, the thud
of it filled my mouth as I stood,
hands in pockets, teeth free of toothpaste.
Father chatted to a high-vis coat,
held a rolled programme in his hand.
Clenched it with Monday morning work.

Plastic cups had steam-shaped hair.
An old man whistled with a pigeon coo
in his throat. Three men laughed at the sun
that tried to sneak onto the pitch.
Corner flags showed the adult world
that comes after school.

Then the players ran off. Plastic seats hid
behind coats, jeans, and stubble. Eye bags
watched the greenness get soaked
by sprinklers. Father sat by us, his lips
full of swear words. I zipped up my coat,
waited for a man to blow a whistle.

Washing Lines

We stretched out a cord to divide us all.
Someone served a cucumber-coloured ball –
it bounced twice until graphite forearms
whacked it back. A neighbour's cat
jumped off a fringe that looked over a fence.
The ball landed in someone's stare.
We asked for it back, but got fed
microwave heat. Swifts bent school
rulers above our heads, squealed away
summer holidays. When they left, a bus
carried us to buildings that ties lived inside.
Someone found chalk and mapped out
a court. Our feet, hemmed in,
lost balance, before a parent showed us
how to swipe flies out of a kitchen.
The game carried on again, each point
fizzed in the cans of coke that stubbed
our teeth. Box hedging gobbled up loose
shots, and we muttered to each other,
found the ball in a Sega game later on.

The Free-Kick

Mother leaned onto the pitch. Her voice crow-shouted
as the players lined up a wall. The goalkeeper frog-leapt.
Painted referee pointed at blades of grass. Some of the studs
changed position. A man in a shirt and tie stood
vicar-still on the sideline. The fans lowered their mouths.

I watched the goalie rub his gloves with a towel.
He wiped a skim of cloud off his forehead. Someone
whispered in his ear, patted him on the behind.
Mother shook her tongue, stubbed out a fag on my head.
Swore at the aeroplane breaking up the silence.

A cough flew around. A sneeze bulleted out of a glass eye.
The other three stands stared at me. I gulped a waft
of hotdog, held my breath until Monster Munch
woke my fingertips. The referee blew his whistle.
A number ten ran towards a mud-smeared ball, hit

it with his shoelaces. The wall of men jumped up
as if evading an incoming tide. Curly-haired goalie
dived into Orion's Belt, his fingers stretched for the join
of post and crossbar. Mother raised her arms,
and everyone around me roared like a burst volcano.

Mother's Hair

Mother walks towards me. Sunlight falls
through her open cigarette packet.

Her arthritic legs stumble like she's walking
a pebbled beach. Conker eyes sprout

as we make contact across the road.
The black hair, greyed, thinned into the pothole

of day to day. We meet on the curb and I see
my childhood escaping her hair. Back home

I check the mirror, see my waning moon scalp.

One More Turn Out Before Jail Term Ended

The last time we went would have been '95.
When school was running out of time and hair grew
on our skin like gorse on a hillside.
This time we smelt the hobs of alcohol, knew nicotine,
heard swear words from adult mouths. A can of Coke
tilted into our mouths to wash away the bacon sarnie
we bought in a peeling-paint cafe. We looked at females too.
Followed the hair colours of our mothers. Smiles
filled our faces, giggles went up into gulls' beaks,
then they let them back out from the top of lampposts.
The sky, a fried onion in a burger van, arcade machines
winked at us and ringed doughnuts teased our phallic brains.
The jail sentence of school lessons was coming to an end.
The stretch of childhood frayed as our muscles started to break
the callus of innocence. Our height stretched up with each
dance song or feral laughter at someone's hairdo.
On this day the road went for miles, and we should've walked
the promenade instead of tying up our wallets. A sun burnt
time until stars poked through as we waited at the train station.
Unaware these days were the last we would ever live.

His Wife was an Electrician

He wore slippers made of duck feathers, drove a Škoda
through the snow, but a Lada in the months of summer.
I never knew if he liked oranges or apples as he ate both
at the same time. His wife an, electrician, fed the house
light bulbs through Pringle tubes. She wired him up
for years, and when he walked, you saw him leaning
on a lamppost as if running out of battery. They were married
for the length of my childhood. He made scones on a Tuesday,
and bread on a Wednesday. Brought them to the local school.
We spread butter with our ironed palms, used Lego teeth
to change the shape of the food in our mouths.
He walked his dog every day with a brown belt for a lead.
His flat cap fizzed with electrodes that his wife planted
in there before he left. If our ball landed in the garden
we knocked with our feet, hoped the rubber soles kept us alive.
He answered through the letterbox, talking out of a tuba mouth.
His wife watched us from the living room window
as we hovered above the lawn. Daffodils grew along borders,
and other plants teachers talked about in springtime lessons.
I knew the colours, but the shapes eluded my empty brain.
We left with quick feet and jumped back onto the earth.

Fossilised Voice

The moon has funnelled away
the sunlight. It holds today's
amber until the clouds paint
it black. The farm field
is waiting for the plough, so I
walk, crunch stalks,
burp puddles. I wait for her
words to flood my ear canal.
The cochlea waits like a seashell
for the tide's song. A wait
of thirty-odd years for the
once-pink tongue now
fossilised in my mind.

05.30

The smoke moves out of the chimney
as a hunting cat's tail. A morning sun
pushes through the clouds like a thumb
in a shoelace loop. Stars are flecks
of chalk off a blackboard eraser.
The dog pulls me into the new frost.
I mutter to her through cow lips.
She looks back, then pulls me further
from home. Hedgerows are moss along
a window sill. I catch my breath in the sugar
of a bowl of Frosties.

A car brings its headlights to the low light,
flushes past as me and the dog stand
on the verge. A female tawny owl shakes out
a call that's been caught in the fur of a rodent.
A neighbour's fog rises out of their garden.
Someone's dog starts to break up the jigsaw
silence. The lead extends my view of the turning
earth. A liquid yellow forms to a cyst of orange,
ignites rooftops, streetlights, clouds.
We walk into the darkness of light, wake up
sleep that lingers in the crust of our eyeballs.

Outer World

The sky was buffalo tongue
with the moon a distant light
yearning to reach the earth.

Someone had forked the sky
leaving holes for the outer
world to shine through.

And I stood whispering

'I miss you, I miss you.'

He Lives Alone with His Wife Next Door

I see him sometimes walking his newspaper up the road.
His hair thatches eyebrows he stole from an aunt lost to cancer.
He does have a wife, though she lives with the neighbour
until he goes to work, then her feet bring her home to bake.
Some say he snores like a whale, and she needs to sleep,
due for reasons no one knows, except a robin that sings in the ivy.
Their house pillars sunlight as bacon fries in the neighbour's pan.
He throws an apple for the seagulls to fight over on his garage roof.
Sometimes she will pop round, grab a kettle of tea before escaping
again, in the shade of potato-stained clouds. They've made love
twice, once on a hammock, and another time on a wheelbarrow.
He said "Never again!" as Sciatica chanted his name for two weeks.
If she comes around when they're both in she shares a photo album
of lost seaside holidays. They both sit with tartan rugs on their laps,
and a grin that stretches the washing line outside.

He is retired these days, allows work to drip from arthritic bones
filling up the avenue's potholes. If you see him early bird song
his eyes squint as if they are wine bar lemons. He once mowed
the lawn with a naked top half. Scars patterned his back
like his life had been sewn together. I have since found out
he was a Japanese POW.

A Quick Drop Off and a Two Metre Distance Chat

We drop off the shopping with parachute hands.
Stand in neighbourly distance. Your energy
runs out of you as a child on waking up at Christmas.
The glass eye dozes as if some of you is still asleep.
You give us photocopied money with your monopoly
fingers. I told you I bought extra tins to give next
week a rest, and us, from the arrows on supermarket
floors, and high-vis coats that point and nod as we cattle.

I told you to walk around the block, shake off the dust
that mother left before she went into a home.
Your hamstrings are tightened by time's screwdriver.
The clock grows louder with each day. A wall calendar
drips away dates you've missed with each kettle boil,
buttered sandwich, press of a remote button.
The living room, a waiting room, an in-between,
and the newspaper pages you turn, drop words down
the phone, when you ring up Mother around tea-time.

A Phone Call Before the Sun Fell off the Earth

I spoke to you last night as I walked the dog
around two fields. My beetroot-stained fingers
smudged the horizon before the sun fell
off the earth. Drought had started to crack the land
as an egg when a chick starts to grow.

Your voice, weak against the television
that nattered in your room. We talked about football,
pets, father, how terrible things were. I watched
a crow paper-aeroplane out of a cloud.

The dog sniffed at the wardrobe air. I told you
we'll meet again late summer, four months earlier
than what I know. I saw your bed palming your life
as you once did with me when I was born.

My voice laboured from the uneven ground.
Your words sounded as if on a flat-back truck
getting ready to move to the next life. We departed,
and I released the phone from my ear. Heard a robin
sing, watched the dog piss against an oak tree.

You're There and I am Here, Wedged by Corona

The ceiling hovers above your head.
Urine drips into a bag, dust, mosses
the top of the wardrobe. Biscuit crumbs
mingle on the overbed trolley.

A fire exit light hums greeness
in the corridor. Nurses walk along
thinning floorboards, waitering bed towels,
mugs of tea, smiles and chit chat.

You lie in the life-wreck of yourself.
Bones, too heavy to lift anymore
muscle condenses into the bed sheets.
Veins pipe themselves against your skin.

I think of all this and more as I sit
at home with only work to go to.
Feel the weight of missed visits
in the phone calls I make when shoeless.

The Boy Who Waits Outside in the Dark

The house lights square off the windows.
A cat sits on a car bonnet. I stand under
the boughs of an oak, listen to my breathing.

The door is closed to keep out the cough.
A sky curves around the town, lampposts shine
on what the day knows.

I rang the number for my mother. She answers
and her voice is light-years in distance, though I
am one hundred yards from where she lives.

I hold a carrier bag, allow the breeze to rustle
out a tent noise from its skin. A note hangs
on the front door, repeats 'No entry'.

I wait with the stars. My tongue balances the weight
of my words as I let each one slip from me,
splash into the puddle that surrounds my feet.

We talk as morning birds. I heard the news on your TV.
Numbers fill my ear canal, drift to my brain, flood.
I wave at the house knowing you are round the back.

And this is what it will be like when the time comes,
and I will wait outside in the dark to see you again.

Getting Older with a Barking Dog

The neighbour has a dog with a puppet shadow-mouth.
It barks until the sun moves to another continent.
I keep the window closed, let Beethoven mingle with dust
that flecks off our skin as snow in a beginning winter sky.
My feet ache, full of work, weighing down streets I know.
I hear the dog nudge its voice through a rattle of a tractor
that shuttles up the road. A cup of tea wafts a thinning hairline
of heat up my nose as I sip with a cat-shaped frown.

The spine I grew as a child bends with a rusty hinge creak.
A blackbird calls from inside my ear, reminds me of Mother's
back garden where the hedgerow blinked sparrow feathers.
I turn on the light, watch shadows fall from ornaments.
A bark runs out of the dog's mouth, rushes to our front window,
taps the glass as a chiffchaff knocking for the month of March.
Tetley yawn forces my jaw to shape itself into a JCB bucket.
The neighbour's garden gate opens, releasing a wagging tail.
I close the curtains, then my eyelids drift to a place I haven't been.

I Walk There Before It Opens

The sky is a thought in my head
as I walk through this pothole sunlight.
A robin decorates the winter hedge,
calls out to the hibernating winds.
My feet, lung-breath with each step.
The church is far enough to sweat,
but close enough to see in the dark.
Stars freckle a cheek of blackness
as white light hoovers up the night.
I hear a cough bounce up my throat,
throw it to the floor as dirty washing.
A car with owl-eye headlights spears
my sleep until I wake up from a dream
that still lingers. The tyres scratch
my skin as we pass each other.
I catch a glimpse of the driver
who sits behind a frown. A pigeon
catapults from a tree; crows peck
a ploughed field in the half-light.
I hear the church bells, though they
hang silent in the tower. I hold
a prayer between my fingers.
A kitchen light keeps a house alive,
streetlights nipple the village up ahead.
I know I'm early, but there's something
in the mouth before words are spoken
that God only hears.

Walking Home in the Rain

The rain pellet-gunned my forehead, stapled clouds
to eyebrows not grown since teenage years.
The road lingered under my feet, fed itself into the dying
sunlight. Leaves whistled themselves to the floor
as autumn shaved away summer. Winter hid
inside letterboxes, bin lids, and conifer hedging.
I walked with a thumb-press of each foot, tried my best
to keep the earth moving. Energy saving light bulbs
painted windows yellow as people gnomed sofas.
Raindrops slid down my nose as children on a slide.
My eyelashes blinked with the cows in the field.
Angry shadows emerged into ink blob darkness.
Cars jumped out of my pocket as I plunged myself
deeper into the clouds. Home was too far away
for me to stop. I turned on my phone's torch,
shook away fox eyes and badger feet. Pinned the moon
into the sky once a corner came. Bullet-walked
down a tunnel of dying rain. Sieved words
people had said to me during the day.
Caught the sight of our rooftop in the clouds' grip.
Punched my way until the door stood in my mouth.
I opened it, saw the dog wagging her tail,
and felt dry land under my feet.

When the Rain Comes By

The rain removes the house from my face,
leaves me with holes to drain my mother's milk.
I walk into this cell of cloud, drop
a whistle from my avenue jaw.
There are daffodils in the mind from yesterday,
when the morning was blood orange
and the moonlight sharpened frost.

The road turtle-shells over earth's cartilage.
Vehicles heave themselves one way, bobsleigh
the other. Blank houses harvest voices,
sky dishes, wooden gates, the community cat.
Button cars woodlouse between kerbs.
The rain is lost. Bounces off the cancerous
dermis as debris in bombing raids.

The bus stop is over this cloud,
but below the next. I keep on walking.
My thoughts noodle my brain,
hashtag the day in the trouser pocket.
Puddles clingfilm the nimbostratus
as I mulch more of the earth into my shoes.
Summer is the time for rain, kettle rain,
that feeds the flowers I cannot name.

This rain has been here since I left the breast,
slid down the pulpit of my youth.
Slapped its grammar on my forehead,
filled socks in phallic-driven years.
Now it soaks the bone in adulthood
waits to become arthritic when greyness settles.
I keep on, push a barrow of my life
into the cloud's osmosis, hear rain gossip fathoms.

A Typical Tradesman that Lives by Us

We see him walking his dog under bat wings as streetlights
blink a body he moves along moss-tired tarmac.
The dog sniffs our fingertips that linger fish and chips.
Sawdust falls from his hands as he starts to retire himself
before age catches him unaware. His smile butters another
Orion's Belt, as the moon pins up a sky he's known
since his father left.

In the avenue, his work van blends into people's curtains.
His dog goes to work with him, sits on the passenger seat reading
a newspaper as they share sandwiches in the petrol station layby.
During the day you hear him saw wood or hammer nails into his head.
I see him sometimes cutting bread with a tenon saw or cleaning
an apple with a pencil rubber. In summer, sunlight slides down
the shed roof, drips onto block paving but his wife sweeps it up
in case the dog lies on it.

His son pops round if the fridge is full. They talk across a measuring
tape, words fill the gaps in the pouring-a-cup-of-tea-silence.
He has a daughter, but someone said she lives with a plumber,
so doesn't visit. I heard him once say his father's last look rests
in the dog's skull like fox eyes caught in torchlight. He retires
next week to allow his life to crumb the living room carpet
and dust ornaments his wife buys from B&M.

A Conversation with an Old Man I Live by

If he stands too long, he'll dwindle into the leaf mould
of his hedge. Paperweight-feet keep him from the pub.
Red veins creep over his nose as cracks in dry soil. He pants
away our conversation before resting again on his garden wall.
I catch a glimpse of his youth in eyelashes that flicker
snowflakes falling off a roof.

We swap clichés with toast-stained teeth, drag a sentence out
of each other as we both want to say how bad things are before
it's too late. I lean away from the promenade that escapes
his memories. Listen to whispered words he pushes into my
ears alongside a neighbour putting out her recycling tubs.

Back home, his wife keeps him up straight, unfolds his wallet
before and after sunlight. In the years since my last death
they've swapped seven cars, changed their dog fur four times,
and kept the same window cleaner since double-glazing went in.
The weight of their love is in the cup and saucer they share
on a Sunday morning after chapel.

He gives me a wink, hints at my disappearing youth, taps
me on the shoulder to see if he's awake.
We walk away, allowing a gap to grow along the tarmac.
I slice the corner, look back, and see him lose another day.

That Moment When the Glass Cracked and We Ran for Our Lives

Vimto fizz sprayed itself off a cloud's forehead as we ran home
in the rain. The cornflake morning became a skinned onion
as our golf ball broke a window on the other side of the field.
Now we ran with galloping legs, sprinter's eyes and a dog's tail.
My heart rolled around my chest as a loose potato in a shopping trolley.
We army-hopped a garden wall, hid behind an apple tree.
Our mouths panted as a kettle after making ten pot noodles.
The sky lowered itself so we knew how far was home.
A car sped past, brakes clinging to the wheels with a forehead
behind the wheel. We checked for safety, then ran again,
headed for the alleyway that's an artery to a lung-space of life.
The golf bag hung off my shoulder. Crossing the Somme was easier.
We'd no idea where he was, or knew who he might become.
Sweat melted off my face. One more road to cross and safety.
A car pinged around a corner; we sipped through lunchtime air,
straightened our backs, wolf-chased our parents' names.
Lawnmowers cut away the summer's fringe, hedge trimmers
grinded at the neighbour's plaque. We chipped over an adult glance,
headed for the houses we knew, pushed through garden gates,
found ourselves with a cracked pane to hide from all summer.

Unusual Phone Call

Her voice is clearer today
when I put the phone to my ear.
Words filter through
like they've never been lost.
It's the mother of years ago
when I grew up with her tongue
while my father worked. The distance
has gone, and we share the same
planet. Her breathing is the wing
beat of an eagle. We talk as child
to parent should, words punch
through the receiver as the first
sunlight on a hill. Back and too
we go, our mouths struggle to keep
up with the pace. Then I say 'Goodbye'
knowing tomorrow her voice
will sound far off and slow
like it has been since I left home.

He Works in a Saw Mill

He wears cinnamon eyebrows found in the school sandpit.
Apple-biting yawn falls out of him each morning
as he rises with a folded newspaper on his chest.
His wife left him years ago, fed up with his whistle.
Now he enters home with junk-mail.

He works in the local sawmill that sits seven corners
from his house. Cuts wood with a tongue shaped
like a shoe insole. Shaves rough edges as he swigs
another can of lemonade. Sometimes he picks up
lost moonlight in his flask, tilts it into a bin for recycling.

After walking home, the smell of sawn wood lingers
in the pit of his stomach. The clattering of timber rabbit-hops
in his ear drums. It keeps him at the toaster for too long,
then burning bread wakes him up, before he spreads jam
via his forehead. He jazz whistles into the fridge.

Two car horn sneezes spray-paint the kitchen floor.
He unfolds his knot-filled skeleton, fills his sandwich
with yesterday's headlines, leaves on the moon
as he turns off the light.

Colin

I see Colin today trimming box hedging with butterfly wing cutters.
Coughing a ten-pound note into the pocket of Levi jeans
he smiles with forgotten teeth, kick-starts cigarettes with Swan Vestas.
The house rises out of the shade, holds up a sky for the cat
to watch birds as they ski across its frayed whiskers.
Colin snips more tufts, pulls out a nettle, grabs sun-dust off
the stone wall below the hedge. He pulls up jeans that are eager
to fall to the floor and scurry away. Tightens a belt not used to being
work-tense. Lost leaves escape a winter breeze as they gather around
his lopsided feet. He pushes the brush across the tarmac,
piles up a summer that cries through decaying flower heads.
In his head, whistling fills empty cavities and ushers away words
he hates to hear. A green bin is filled with the detached, then he knocks
the door of our neighbour. The neighbour swaps him a handshake.
They pass drips of noise off tongues painted with middle age.
A take-away laugh bellies out of Colin before he pats the neighbour
on the shoulder, walks with a rake in his hand, grabs his coat off a gate,
swings it over a shoulder that's fettered with arthritis and lie-ins.

The Wood Chopper

He chops logs with yesterday's face. Grimaces against a sunlight
that shows who he is. Sweat grows from under his skin,
fills the leaf mould with dampness. The axe thumps into the tree,
punches its way until a triangular wound is created.
Sap is shocked on the bark. Leaves rummage with each blow.
Birds twitter through broken beaks. Clouds wait for the ground
to open up. He swings again, forces muscles to turn his body
as a screw into a knot. Each whack, the mouth contorts
into a telephone wire being blown in the wind. A creak saws
through the air. He runs back, hears a crash of branches
scrape at the wood it's known. His hand flicks a lighter,
a flame stands against the sunlight, staggers to the end
of a cigarette. Silence fills the vacuum of the wood.
He kettle-click tuts and notices his axe lying under the tree.
Pushes back hair too long for a comb, wipes away
what he's seen, from eyebrows too brown to reflect in a wet conker.

I Watched Him Take Down a Tree

He saws the blackbird song in half as he talks down a tree.
The crash of fall flicks up leaf matter, and lost sunlight.
His flat cap balances on his skull as if plate spinning.
I watch him through leaves bullet-holed by wind and rain.
An oak branch covers me in shade until I blend into the bark.

He carries on, unaware of my sitting or the sky, that's held up
by trees he's cutting down. His mouth gobs a molehill,
pollutes puddles that rain has brought in the night.
Chainsaw glimmers sap like a crow with morning frost.
Clouds fill the sun's face, spread my shade further into this wood.
His Land Rover sits in the stuffed stillness. Six jackdaws pass
two notes to each other as they fly overhead. He looks up,
woodpeckers their flight with a mimic of a gun.
The tree lies on the wind it's crushed on the way down.

He scratches mud off his boot onto a seasoned pine of oak.
Snaps a branch with dirty hands. Throws away loose growth
until spring is lost in the standing trees. A flask is poured
out of his mouth, fills up divots he brought with his boots.
He blends his face with the ripped-out roots of the felled tree.
Breaks a chocolate bar in half, shapes its wrapper into a sparrowhawk.
Sits back against the wood's light, grinds up crusts for waiting birds.
Stabs a hand into pockets like a stoat in a rabbit burrow.
Pulls an extra finger, lights up his pipe, filling the new sky with smoke.

He Came Round One September Week
to Fix a Roof

You can go to him for advice, but not when he speaks.
His belly fits into a tumble dryer drum. Smoke lingers
between the gaps in coffee-stained teeth. I hear the saw
grind against knots that are worn into his bones.
There's a light behind each eye, maybe shines, or dims
with each drag of his rollie. Carrot-baton fingers, tender
enough to flick newspaper pages, but hide strength
that breaks the morning silence. His saw butters my toast
as I scrape lost dreams onto callused bread. The dog sniffs
the air knowing he is filling up our outside space.

He laughs a cough and has a scoff of a Tesco-bought scone.
Then fixes a roof that leaks winter all year round, though
it keeps summer above the sky like the umbrella Mother once
used to take me to school. A grinder cuts a tobacco earth
in two and I hear a melon-like roll. He talks to the neighbour,
pots words into her ears to melt her clay wax. They mutter
as two crows that sit on telephone posts in a sky-fed field.
Tap-tap-tap goes the hammer as he knocks a nail through
his past. Dust falls to a slab erroned floor as slug trails carry
last night's starlight. He works until sandwiches tell him
to go home. A phone call off his wife carries along the road
as I walk the dog with her tree-scented nose. Already the moon
is a hammock in the sky as we both hope he's gone on return.

The Joiner Next Door

He cuts wood with a terraced-house hand. Holds a cigarette
until it burns away. The smoke greys his hair.
He has no clock, or a wife, to cook him a Sunday roast.
The dog lies in the shade of flower pots full of annuals.
Shavings cover a concrete floor as he wipes council sweat
off his brow. There's a sun in the sky that boils an old kettle
with two cups of tea for lunch. He rubs ointment into marriage
wrinkles. Spits out last night's whiskey. Age has shocked
the hell out of his eyes. Four handkerchiefs fist a jean pocket.
Each one used for different parts of his skull. A tenon saw
holds moonlight in its teeth, two hacksaws gather memories
from childhood days with a granddad he never knew.

The wood clatters the spinning earth, wakes up three sparrows
in his eyelashes. His mouth sniggers, smiles, burps sawdust
into the conifer hedging. He follows the pencil line to cut
a length of pine as the oven cooks a pie. Sixteen moves
of his arm brings out blackboard shade off his shed roof.
He gasps for air. Pulls a cigarette from a toolbox, lights
it with a match struck off the back of a photo of his wife.

RSPB Conwy During Covid-19

We went today, visited a sky that shuffled clouds from its bottom draw.
Seagulls coordinated the motorway and mountains. Cars hobbled into
the car park from the zip-wire tarmac. We waited for people to distance
from our breath so we could gasp our own words.

The estuary had been pulled into the sea's mouth. Curlews punched
sand, searched for yesterday or last millennia. Oystercatchers lit up
their beaks with their awareness. Cormorants brought the Jurassic,
showed us what earth will become again when we die.

Hides locked up; we're left to moments of hope between the gape
of land and sky. I've never seen the world as open as today. The prefrontal
cortex closed allowing me to wander through a catalogue of thought.

Small birds fired themselves out of shrubs or hedgerows. Little egrets
stood in vicar coats, tried their best not to print the sand with their weight.
Coots and moorhens floated as commas in a drowned book.

Mid-Twenties

Sometimes on a Saturday we are ferried out
on the white horse and a rattling train.
We sing territory songs, fill stations with pigeon-clucks.
The Old Bill follows. Our shoulders dip in and out
of the sunlight. Rockport shoes stamp away the dust
of this town. Some of us mould our hands into fists,
grind them into snarling dogs. The sky is somewhere,
and the trees I know are left behind at home.
A gate is opened and we cattle move.
Ten men shout from across the road. We jump up
like puppies at feeding time. Seagulls flick off
lampposts, pull in the clouds. The police extend batons,
hold them up as teachers with rulers when explaining
Pythagoras. People leave the train station,
watch us line up behind a wall of dried fruit faces.
A helicopter pops up out of a beer can. The ten men
are pushed down the road. Their bull heads fade back
into a pub where they will stare from behind cracked glass.
The police let us move, feed us with nods and glances.
The white horse gallops up the road through shopping centres,
around cars and passed burger vans. Our heads, terraced
by the plastic chairs we have to sit on. We all jabber,
forget the game, watch the police helicopter that tries
to hide inside a hotdog.

Sitting in My Book Shed

I look through the window, notice slug trails shaped around
a distant winter tree. My body boils out my breath.
A casing of a spider hangs off a splinter. Cobwebs fill
in gaps between books. My gasping hair
tries to cover my head before the winds pick up.
The page is turned again for words to ferret into a brain
shaped like a boot. I mould who I am around verbs,
and a simile found in a sweet wrapper. A draught squeezes
through the gap in my mouth, feeds sentences
I'm yet to write. Birds flick across my pupils,
move my head free of dust. A something runs
under the carpet. Titles drip off the bowing shelves,
fade from the morning sunlight. I think of the dog
indoors as she waits, her lead clenched between
her two meals a day. The dishwasher needs emptying,
oven trays scrapheap themselves on the drainer.
A bill waits to be paid, though eager to add interest.
DMs are somewhere on a phone that lies asleep.
The cats mingle within their fur, wait for a rodent
to turn them into animals. I sigh another line
of poetry, let it run along my tongue as the tractors
that pass by our house.

A Morning Jog on a Road Only I Know

The clouds scuffle with the morning sunlight.
I am upside down with a world shaped like a headache.
Sheep pin cushion fields of yesterday's summer.
I hit the tarmac with heavy knees, catch a buzzard
sitting on two fence posts. Feel last night drip
out of the joints I grew in the gym as a teen.
A shiver falls between me and the road.
My breath silvers a horizon yet to burst open
as the sky stays ajar to allow nightmares to leave.
Purrs from our kitten pass by in rotating car tyres.
The main road keeps me hemmed from the loudness.
A security light beams from a barn, gives sheep a grey
shade that nudges away their fading white.
In the distance, a town lies asleep with lit fags of streetlights.
I make sure to turn back when our road is done,
unsure if reaching deeper into old memories
will get me further.

A Walk in the Rain

There's gull rain outside and it weighs down leaves.
I put my boots on and take an afternoon walk.
A lapwing oars the field's sky as it comes in for spring.
Black blobs of jackdaws speckle the low crop field.

A squirrel races through the branches, tries to catch up
yesterday. Puddles gather around me. But I keep on
walking. This road leads somewhere though
the cambers ache away my energy.

I keep on going. I hope to find the end.

The Horseshoe Falls

From above the main road
the river had become foil.
I walked along limestone
and tufts of grass. The sun
started to set alight the gorse,
and wheatears flicked between
grey and silver rocks.
I ventured to the canal, followed
the conveyor belt of water.
I noticed the river had caught up
and started to grow from below.
The gushing of erratic currents
sounded like a radio between
stations. The canal slicked on,
but the river climbed higher.
Until the Horseshoe Falls
linked them both. I sat by an oak.
Listened to the in-between of
nature and man-made water courses.
And saw myself in both lanes,
so, I went to Llantysilio church,
and asked God to pick my current.

We Did This and We Did That

Me and 'T' ran shopping centres.
We sewed extra pockets inside our coats,
funnelled stuff into our lives without paying.
Shop shelves showed white panels,
peg hooks looked lonely. It was a simple game,
he walked in and fell over a basket. I followed,
filled my pockets with this and that.
He walked out with a limp and bandage
I sat on a metal seat whistling songs from my youth.
He once pinched a set of dumbbells
and we struggled through town carrying the weight.
He bought me Fruit Pastilles to say sorry, because my
arms were dead for a week. For six years
our reign emptied the town we were born in.
Then one day he accused me of stealing something
of his. He said I had taken it from him and he
would never get it back. I was upset. He ripped
out his extra pockets and threw away his coat.
I sat on the bench turning back the hands of my
watch. He never looked at me again or his mum
who knew what we had been doing since school.
I asked him what he thought I had taken
and he replied, 'My youth.'

They Have Never Known Him

They fished at the side of his brain, searched
for who he was when the moon corked.
Some said he lived as a bull in a field
snorting and sighing all day.

One person told him to get on with his life
as he hadn't done much. Another mentioned
to take drugs, drink beer and watch porn.
Others smiled at him when he went to town.

People talked when drunk, shredded his name
over the bar. Poured out his initials
with shots of vodka. Chewed his past
inside a kebab on walking home.

He knew this as when he got up in the morning
parts of him were missing. As he walked
downstairs to let the dogs out he grew
back what he'd lost. Smiled at his face

in the morning frost that mirrored the sky.

Skin

When he left his skin behind in town
the others rubbed their chins.
He felt the earth on his flesh, heard
the words he had spoken leave in the wind.

The others picked up his skin,
tore pieces off and put it in their wallets.
They paid for beer with what they stole,
threw away the rest with spit.

When he came back, they hid from him
in case he wanted his history back.
But when they saw him on the street
he'd grown another dermis.

The others looked at their phones to see
if he had called their numbers.
When they saw he hadn't, they carried
on walking, turned corners before he did.

Winter Solstice

When the earth becomes a jug
and tilts away the summer's sun
I'm left with shadows and owls.

Winter hibernates trees, blows
away seeds, falls down chimney
pots. Darkness stretches out,

holds back the light. I walk into
tunnels, squeeze my way through
the weather. There's an open door

in the sky allows winds to brush
away what I know, have grown.
The sun hauls itself to the parapets

and gables, holds the towns and cities
in its weakest noon. Then curtains
close before I'm home and a light bulb

turns my ceiling to a summer sky.

Released from the Four Walls

Back when we were kids spring chased summer
as the earth's pottery wheel turned below our feet.
Trees posed for our eyes as we tip-topped to the woods.
Branches became our bones as each journey stretched
us further into the emptiness. Sheep yawns moulded
our morning faces, crow saliva gobbed from a mouth
we didn't use in our radiator school lessons.
Brambles shocked fingertips, nettles, pylon-fuzzed
shin bones, cow pats made us hop-scotch.
The sky opened up as a market stall canopy,
and we sensed the nature within. Unknown birds
flicked off our eyelashes, insects turned us to jungle
warfare. Butterflies increased cordial sunlight.
The river went through our ear canals, barbed wire
clung to T-shirts, kissing gates clapped us
to the next path. Wildflowers mingled on our faces
until we went to sleep. The heat of the sky
pressed down onto us, left patches of redness
that made our mothers tut when we got home.
Voices gargled the river's current, pebbles
skimmed the water's passing. Our silly jokes
snagged to parents' eyebrows as they pushed prams,
and led dogs from one shit to another.
Everything in the woods on this day came out of us
in adulthood, arthritis, fluttering, darkness and decay.
Jumping a stile, a foil milk bottle top became the moon
as we slurped the last white cloud of the day.

The Sky Showed Me

I raked the soil with metal spider legs
caught a ladybird in flight with my eyes.
I tried to turn over winter, start again.
A buzzard stirred the sky.

A spade leaned itself against a wall.
The wheelbarrow waited to catch rain
as I hoped to let things dry out.
Gulls stretched the sky.

I heard seventeen syllables
and headed inside for dinner,
leaving behind hours of work.
Feathered clouds whitened the sky.

Later, when I came back outside,
grease from the fish made me rub
my fingers on my trousers.

Sunlight spread itself across the bottom
of space. I heard the sun break
winter that lay in the plastic guttering.
There was a release somewhere,

and the sky curved itself around the earth
as a hand holding an orange. I escaped.